DUNES REVIEW

DUNES REVIEW
VOLUME 21, ISSUE 1

FROM THE EDITOR

It's an honor to share with you my first issue as editor of a journal I'm proud to say is now one generation — many seasons — old. As I write during the turn of winter to spring, when pools pinhole the frozen lakes, the theme of change occupies my mind. Reading through the newest incarnation of this journal, I wonder: *What can writing change?*

The pleasure of writing, for myself, and, hopefully others, lies in its ability to help us reconceive our beliefs about the figures and things in our lives. Wildlife we think we've domesticated over the centuries, for instance, may not be what it's always seemed. "All pets are imposters," according to Andrew Szilvasy. Writing also has the power to subvert age-old symbols; Elizabeth Kerlikowske describes cleaning lightbulbs that don't look like ideas.

Let's also see writing, then, as a testing ground for invention — for fresh situations and ideas. How about Michael Bartelt's proposing Walt Whitman as moderator of the presidential debate? And how would it feel to lord over a package of miniature people? Johnathan Greenhouse explores.

Through such explorations, writing portrays new states of being. Catherine Anderson movingly conceives of injury as "a public stillness held inside." And in another look at injury, we find imaginative ways to manage pain when it surfaces. Petra Kuppers fashions a protagonist faced with a decision on breast-cancer treatment who takes a rejuvenating dream-swim with a troll.

What we seek then, through literature, is a means of perceiving anew — the daily, the safe, the hopeless, the dormant, the tiny. May you experience, many times over in reading this issue, what John F. Buckley calls "a mouselint epiphany."

Yours,
Tanya Muzumdar

5

DUET

she swings the tube	he curls his lips
once a vulture's wing bone	around the knife-skinned reed
to her embouchure	once a hollow of cane
twirls air down the cylinder	warming the ebony
out to the concert hall	down through the bell
where it breaks	free of the instrument to
the cavern of silence	the front row gaze
the dancing flutist	the swaying clarinetist
pipes altissimo	murmurs chalumeau
silver keys click	a whispered intimacy
the tones shimmy	up arpeggios
twist round each other	in strands, braids weaving
a design, a pattern	until the audience becomes
what it all means	what the mingled notes draw out
the feelings released	from their moorings
to change the color	shades of white
refracting from the flute	to the dimmed chandelier
to the listeners	bones aglow

TO THE STORY GIRL

She surely rose to magnificent heights
of insane fury of effort bred of her terror
of me. —William Carlos Williams

The doctor painted your portrait
in words: golden locks, fever's flush.
He told how you clawed
at his eyes, knocked glasses
from his face to keep him
from knowing your truth —
your throat coated
in scarlet. Prying
your clenched teeth,
he thrust the stick,
which you splintered.
Your mother shook
you by the arm. Pinning
you down, your father heard
your shriek, loosened his grasp.
I wanted to climb
into the pages. I wanted
you to tell me how you came
to have a voice.

REBECCA OET

ENDGAME TACTICS

I grabbed my father
    from a city of fathers,
snatched
    his cow-leather hands.

There's a skeleton face sticker,
    winking at me from the ceiling.
Between the curtains the
    air is smudged.

His head is hazard and light,
    looking up at the turquoise moon.

Have I prisoned him in layers of chessboards?
    Pawns are flying, the rooks have vanished,
    and it seems the queen has
lost her crown.

Tiptoeing into a haze
    of limping eyelids,
    have I condemned him?

PATRICIA CLARK

IT'S STILL FATAL

I saw my ex-husband in a hotel lobby. He was with a group of conference people and smiled broadly, unlike in the past. I knew his secret of false teeth. He could appear confident in his black leather jacket with the collar up. I wasn't fooled.

"Hello, my pet," he said, swinging my way across the gleaming floor. Long ago, I'd heard from mutual acquaintances that he had a new wife and also dogs.

I said, "No pet of yours. It's the full Susanna now." I used to go by "Sue."

The check-in clerk behind the glossy counter said, "Photo ID and credit card, please."

I was bothered by the over-strong smell of lilies. When I turned, there they were—Asiatic ones, pink fleshy blossoms, freckled, and bright stamens with cinnamon-colored pollen. In huge gold vases, three, spaced along the counter.

"A quiet room," I said, "Not near the elevator."

My ex followed me across the lobby where I spoke to the concierge. "Yes, Thai food, I think. And within walking distance." In his cap and uniform, the concierge nodded. Then he handed me the folded area map and brochures about harbor tours.

"Who are you with?" my ex asked.

I attend this annual conference, in publishing, a field we share. Me as author, he as agent.

"I don't need company, Alex." Curt, appropriate. I wheeled my burgundy and black carry-on behind me, zipped into a just-closing elevator, and was down the hall, sliding the room card out to the green light, when I heard the room phone ring.

"Remember that restaurant in Houston, right off Westheimer?" He always had a long memory.

"The one with the string lights shaped like chili peppers?" I thought I could see them.

"Exactly." He paused and I suppose we were both in that place, back twenty plus years ago in memory. I stared at the framed art above my bed, a pseudo Georgia O'Keefe in a garish orange.

A scene came back to me of that very restaurant and Alex proposing marriage. Ridiculous now to think how excited I had felt. A small ceremony a few months later, at an author's house,

10

with a justice of the peace who made house calls officiating. Too far to travel, we justified, no one from his family or mine invited.

"You never invited my father to dinner," he said now. Our minds and words sometimes echoed each other even after years.

"Whitey? I couldn't stand him. Do you remember him insulting me when I told him I wrote about child trafficking? 'Deserve what they get.'"

"Meet me for a drink," he was insisting now—his voice purring like in the old days. "I've got news to share."

I hung up my clothes, put underwear and bra in the small flat dresser drawer, stowed running shoes and gear in the bottom of the closet. My husband would want to know I'd arrived safely so I called—two time zones back.

"Go on to bed," I told him. "I'm here at the hotel just fine. And it's raining." I consciously didn't mention Alex. Why worry my guy? "Love you, sweetie!"

The receiver back in place, I picked up the embossed hotel stationery there by the blotter on the desk. How odd! It came back to me—a folded half sheet that said Vancouver Sheraton with my name in black ink on the outside of an envelope, slipped under a hotel door. 1532. It was here in Vancouver at a different hotel a year or so ago. The mutual friend of the ex and me—someone I ran into at breakfast—and the note simple, "I don't know if you heard, but Alex had to have open heart surgery."

Maybe that's what Alex wanted to tell me about. I lay on the bed now, resting my head on the pillow. Cold, I thought, it's cold in here. I pulled up the coverlet, slipping off my shoes, to rest for just a few minutes. Once I hit fifty-five years old, my feet ached by mid-afternoon. With eyes closed, I saw Whitey, almost shuddering when I remembered his trafficking comment. A short man, he had a tight round protruding belly. And beady eyes like a ferret. He lived with Alex's mother in a double-wide, Arizona. Maybe he noticed me looking around on our one visit: Lay-Z-Boy chair, check, beer (cans) in the fridge, check, no reading material, check. I hadn't been dismissive, even in my mind, till the racist comments and other language.

I was long past blame or hurt. It had been twenty-five years. Still, something vague tugged at me—some surprise of sympathy bubbling up for Alex. Was it for his surgery, or the earlier AIDS scare after a transfusion? He who had railed against gay men, even saying, "They deserve what they get. I hope they all die."

How far can the apple fall from the tree? And then poor hygiene: he had false teeth by thirty-five years old. Dope-smoking, candy, a prescription drug habit.

Downstairs an hour later, I could see his head and jacket when I came around the corner of the bar. Alex stood up, "Oh, let's get a table."

All suave and confident. An act, I thought again. Remember how nervous he got before every social encounter? And before our wedding. Called it "nerves." Him asking me to ask our friends for Valium. I'd had the sense to say no. "You ask!"

"So you're going to a Thai place for dinner?" I could tell he still wanted to hang out. He kept looking around—was he worried about someone seeing us together?

I lied, "Yes, meeting some friends at 7."

"Look, I wanted you to know I had surgery. A blocked artery. And now I have breathing troubles, COPD. Not all the time but just occasionally." He lifted his drink, sipping, the ice knocking. "Smoking really did hurt my lungs. Glad I quit when I did."

Curious, this, both the disclosures from him and the looking back. I didn't know if it was a ploy for sympathy (and maybe I'd relent and include him for dinner), or it was simply our shared past—though it had been only four or five years of togetherness.

I could see our Houston flat, peeling paint on the ceiling. Rituals of Friday night dope smoking, eating Twix bars. How many bad habits had both of us had? When you're young, you think, "no big deal." It was our late twenties, early thirties. Both finishing grad school. In two years, we'd be history to each other.

"Is Whitey still alive?" I wanted to keep the conversation on safe subjects, old stuff.

"Oh god, no. He's been gone ten years." He lifted a finger to signal the waitress.

"My brother has a brain tumor." I said this calmly, letting the words sink in.

"Do you mean Steve?" He coughed, then fumbled at his right pocket for a small inhaler he pulled out. "Excuse me."

"Since he's the only brother I have, yes, . . ." I paused. Steve is my twin, my lawyer brother who never left Seattle.

"They can operate." His voice was normal again. It always bugged me when he'd sound like an expert.

"No, in fact they can't." I was picking at a loose thread on a button at my cuff. Tempted to just yank the damn thread.

"Well, radiation then."

"Sure, but it's still fatal. He'll be gone by. . ." What month was this any way; oh yeah, holidays over; this was January. "He'll be lucky to make it to May." Or would that be lucky? I could see my brother's unsteady walk, his right foot dragging in a brown slipper. I could see his blank eyes.

He was staring. "I like your hair with those streaks. It's good to have hair, isn't it?" He patted his own. He had had a habit in the past of putting me down, over and over. Comments like "Did you do something to your hair?" Or: "Gee, I think those pants add about five pounds to your waist." One time I told him I was feeling down, and he chanted at me in a mocking way, "Sue is blue, Sue is blue." Maybe that was gone. Was he more kind?

Now he said, "Should I order us an appetizer? I'm starved."

"What about a harbor tour tonight, Alex, what do you think?" His eyes widened.

"But the water: won't there be swells? You know I get seasick." He actually looked a bit green already. I knew he wouldn't come.

It was a reflex of mine, this pushing people away, saying I had dinner plans when I didn't. I desired some company; now I could feel that, and it was like food hunger but somewhat different, a different synapse. I felt at peace. I had made the overture. Only half listening now, I could hear him saying how he'd gotten sick once on a boat, how he didn't like leaving shore. I tuned him out.

I desired a plan and in my mind one formed: I would put on my running shoes and go out for forty minutes. A hot shower later, I would find the Thai restaurant and eat alone. I desired now to go on the harbor tour either alone, if Alex didn't come as I suspected, or maybe with someone else tomorrow when the weather might be more fair. Perhaps someone from the conference would go. I desired to have a sympathetic soul. Could wishing for more sympathy help me gain more?

My heart went out to Alex, and to me. He was chewing and talking while I was thinking, and I wondered how his gums were holding up, if he ever had those false teeth adjusted. We were going to die. We were going to have to face it, together and alone. We clinked our glasses, "To friendship," he said, and I concurred. And then we ate the sautéed button mushrooms, one at a time like golden pills, like antibiotics to protect us from what would come.

PETER KRUMBACH

DEATH AT THE OPERA

The stout soprano floats across the stage
like a brocaded weather balloon, eyes of peacocks
on her chest. A whiff of opium, the mind ripples,
you slump next to your wife in the velvet seat.
The air spawns wet pearls, dark
blue, plum, pink...

You find yourself slicing dates into a white bowl.
Apple cut into four green boats, the seeds stunned
by light. The knife blade under running water.
No sound in the afterlife but the chirr
of the insane cricket who fell in
through the glare.

You pour tea into the cup, look at the wan girl
who may be Marie Antoinette. She feeds
the two wrens atop the powdered loaf of her hair,
spoons soft-boiled egg into your mouth.
The cricket trills beneath her hoopskirt,
smooth yolk on your tongue.

She walks you to an orchard where old men
in linen suits point their canes at clouds.
Far from the curtain call, the whisper of your wife,
you're no longer the husk of a man in seat twenty-seven
who now appears to have lost count of the times
he's circled the sun.

JOHN F. BUCKLEY

WATERCRESS ON CRUSTLESS WHITE

Ball gown in fists, she journeyed to Zingerman's
and swung wide her telescope, scanning the faces
for Pippa and Kate. Subterranean nonsense.
She buried her spyglass in a vacant socket
and surveyed the thick crowd at the counter.
With lines so densely packed, how can they insert
the diacritical marks? What about the Bosnians?

Her doppelgänger, a willful plumber from Pontiac,
had already swept the floor of thick, black loam
of cheese rinds and bread crumbs, had already
ordered a Montreal smoked-meat Reuben,
had already found love, taken a bite, and
sent it back for further toasting.

In the deli the women come and go,
looking for a seat on the patio.

David? David? #13, Sherman's Sure Choice, sour pickle?
The server marched through the dining area,
burning and razing all he could find
on the way to the Huron River. For months to come,
survivors would be found huddled below tables
at the farmers market. Some would nibble
stray vegetable samples. Others, hardier specimens,
would return to school to learn a practical trade.

In Angell Hall the candidates lock eyes and act wary,
assessing questionable emotional investment in the work of
     Ashbery.

It's like picking morning-glory seeds from your teeth.
They sighed. Harry flushed the toilet in the third stall
and caused the entire building to rumble and thrash.
There were no more paper towels,
not on the shelves at Tesco's, not in the linen closet,
not until the orb once again reached perihelion.

Flowers cheered and people, each fleshy capsule
in his or her best zippered quilt, cracked open
their codpieces and strewed brightly colored pollen;
it was a Western Holi. Springtime was here,
and all the sandwiches in the realm could not
detract from the heliotropic buoyancy.

Gob shave our gracious bean!
Long lave our hopeful bean!
She waved from the roofs of Detroit Street,
ball gown hung from a stick like a banner.

BUCKET LIST

To touch the flame to the spray again, for
old time's sake. To hook the eye of a young,
thin one passing too close. To draw a black
seed pentagram and call the crows down on
its points. To leave my shoes smelling of cloves
at the end of the promenade. To pierce
my ear with a needle threaded with my
lost darling's hair. To ricochet among
the dancers on the icy wooden floor.
To rock, no, rocket. To sing, coo, gently
remonstrate despite the urge to approve
and be approved. To gather the D&D dice
and derringer for Russian-roulette Yahtzee.
To win the maroon brooch in long-distance
competitive napping. To rearrange
the bodies to spell the menu's daily
specials. To lip a policeman. To hurl
my feats against the front window, leaving
trickling greasy silhouettes. To polish
a mirror until my image weakens.
To recall each chalkstroke of the dwarven
frescoes, the ruffling images on low
stucco walls. To pucker my face against
the onslaught of the past. To doff my hat
in the service of a higher cause. To
surf a proud man's spittoon. To topple and
reach the water. To spend a perfect year
and place it in a box. To haul the small
potatoes inward, to the center, for
the trapped miners. To guide my echoes to
a fresh understanding, a stiff mountain's
farthest peak, a mouselint epiphany.

OF COURSE, YOU CAN'T ACCEPT
THIS APOLOGY, EITHER

If I were an earnest man, I would hold
you above my head in the inundated

sunlight, I would lift you
toward the crenellations
of a vast canon, at least out

of the moat and into
a coracle filled with salmon
and hideously wise anglers, but

the pressure in my gut threatens
to burst from the strain, so we stay

soppy together, passing gas and time
and poorly handrolled cigarettes, two

saltines almost afloat in a potage
of inappropriate spices and vivid

pimentos, unsafe crackers baffled
by even the simplest locks of hair, the curl
of a finger, the slippery yoke of blue oxen.

Somewhere a hermit casts runes in the desert.
Somewhere an eagle flies business class,
launch codes secure in its talons.

Somewhere the populace, prudent enough
to be daunted, sandbags the banks, and none
of my ensuing nonsense would pass.

PETRA KUPPERS

FJORD POOL

The fjord city clasped the shiny rim of the pool at night. A troll pool, designed for large flat-footed creatures with curly hair. The hallway from the showers to the pool is empty and dark. Set into the hallway walls are round observation windows, full of blue light: the pool from beneath, tunnels to see the swimmer creatures on their lines, beetles webbing their way across black bars and blue waves.

In the nascent blue sheen of night, the trolls come out. They roll down the hill, over the mountain, dip into oily lakes deep beneath the crust. They shake their matted hair in the fjords, mini tsunamis worrying widows in their coastal huts. They climb into the 5o-meter pool of Toyen Badet, Oslo's public bath, and launch themselves cross-wise against the lengths, jump high and land on their bellies, laugh at the tickle and dunk down.

Astrid remembered her aunt telling her troll stories, when they had sat side by side in the kiddie pool. Her aunt had her legs drawn up under her, kneeling lightly in the warm water. Astrid had jumped up and down, the water still reaching under her armpit. She must have been five, then, or younger. Now, she still sat in the warm pool at the end of her lengths, and let her legs float out under her. The shimmer of the water was cut by the diagonal of the ramped entry way, a collage of angles and lines converging. Its angularity pleased Astrid's eye.

Her auntie had held her up to the blue holes in the walkway below the pool, and they had stared, together, at the swimmers, at the light, at the magic of observation itself. And later, Astrid had seen televised swim events from this pool, saw again the magic round underwater eyes capturing graceful landings of jumpers, the entry of bubbles and splash. The perspective made her cry, stifle a little sob, and then she remembered her aunt's stories of trolls and other mountainfolk going for a swim.

She cupped a handful of water, let it run out over her knees, warming the cooling flesh. Today, she had to decide about the operation. Would she give up these hillocks sprouting on her chest? She squeezed her hill country between her upper arms. Familiar, and ticklish: not at all dangerous, riven with deep secrets, probed and biopsied. She could go full hog, radical clear-cutting, or decide to go with the lumpy story, the bits and pieces. Hours before she saw her doctor, and her mind still wasn't made up.

She launched herself sideways in the kiddie pool, let gravity take over her body's trajectory in the shallow water. She twirled, twisted, felt the tug of skin where skin's elastic offered counter-pull. The glory of her treasure, her hoard. Astrid whispered to herself the troll secrets, the jewels under the hills.

Beneath her, the seams of tile fluctuated, small streams of bubbles heating under a dragon's breath. Astrid kept twirling, shooting sideways, feeling the strength of her leg muscles, thighs powerful like small horses. Each time her feet punched into the tiles, a little bit more gave, a crack of opening, dilation. She still hadn't noticed the changes on the pool floor. The clock kept ticking.

Her aunt, no longer able to pull her legs beneath her. Unstable. The awkwardness of the bath chair, rolling down the kiddie pool ramp. For a while, they could still go to the public bath together. Then, her aunt's skin had cracked, continents adrift in dry lost deserts. After that, her mind had leaked, gone fuzzy at the edges, in ways that a teenager could only find frighteningly unclear. Astrid wondered about how she would know her aunt's story now, with her own feet anchored firmly in the world.

Astrid dolphin-ducked her way across the shallow warm pool, her back's muscles lifting and arcing her through the waters. Her mind's eye was still far in the past, so she didn't notice the buckling of the tiles in rhythm with her own undulation.

Then she turned, and floated on her back, aware of her breasts spreading out over her chest, spilling like warm dough over the sides. The same, and separate: she already was taking so much more note of these skin sensations, the little feedback from gravity and posture, stuff that would have been far in her unconscious even as recently as two weeks ago. Bodies change. She seal-rolled, side, side, side, side, shift, lift, flutter.

The pool floor erupted beneath her. A pressure wave moved her sideways, pitched her into an eskimo-roll. She handled it fine, her body feeling no need to panic, just a duck and weave, then upward. Her head broke through the warm water, and she looked around, alert, her fear catching up with her diaphragm. She hiccupped and stared. In the middle of the shallow kiddie pool at Toyen Badet, a troll had taken up residency. She, for she seemed feminine, was hairy all over, with slightly chlorinated water now dripping clear out of her fur – no mud on this gal. The hair was shiny and looked soft, and it draped her generous body in waves and folds. A giant nose peeked out of a waterfall of locks. She blew through thick rosy lips, and the hair rose upward as if on a giant hairdryer, floated, and then blew over her head, cascading downward again. Now the nose was freed and it shone even more rosy in the middle of multiple folds, a face wrinkled and strangely young-old. Astrid found it hard to hold on to any fear or even consternation. The troll looked friendly, cheeky, maybe mischievous, but hardly malevolent. She unglued her booty from the pool floor, and duck-eeled her way over to the giant.

The giant responded, elegantly swishing a large hand through the water, as if tracing Astrid's outline. Astrid, in turn, ducked under and planed like an arrow through the blue. The water was a bit higher now, as the troll had displaced quite a bit, and seemed to be blocking with her ass any outflow. This was more fun! Astrid banked, breathed, and went under again, slingshooting off the troll's back pelt. The troll leaned back, into the wave created by Astrid's cresting form. The troll opened her mouth, and laughed. The far distant concrete ceiling shook in response vibration, but held safe and firm. The troll let herself fall back, so the water created a rim all around her. Astrid swam this ring, darting in and out of the fjords of the troll's dark brown soft and undulating body.

So they played, water mediating between them, large and small, mountain and salmon. Eventually, Astrid tired, and the troll held out a large lined hand. Astrid crawled inside, rolled up, and the troll blew on her, drying her, breath strangely sweet and smelling of salmiak licorice. Then the troll deloused her. At least that is how it felt to Astrid, lying still. As the procedure unfolded, she began to hold herself in a ball a bit more stiffly, for some inkling of danger made its way through the layers of curled child pleasures that engulfed her. Large horny nails shifted Astrid's folds and valleys, plucked her bathing suit right off her, tearing and discarding the bits. Astrid looked over the hand's rim, saw the purple flakes of suit rain down a long way to the pool's surface. Then the horned pincers returned.

Night fell over the pool. Far down, on Oslo Fjord, a large

cruise-ship cast off its lines, and headed out into the darkening sound, a lowing ship's horn blast echoing across the harbor. Astrid awoke, stiff and cold on hard tile. What had happened? She was shivering, and found herself naked underneath her sheltering hands. Her skin felt raw in places, scabby even, as if she had been dragged behind a truck over a country road. She welled those fears: she was still in the pool building, safe, and breathing. She was also alone. The troll had gone. In front of her, the kiddie pool lay placid and still. She stood up, stacked her vertebrae one on top of the other, found all muscles responding and willing, if creaking. She walked to the main pool, and looked down into the clear water. The round observation globes in the depth glowed gently back at her, shimmering. She tested the main pool with her toes: colder than the kiddie pool, but acceptable to her achy chill self. She looked around once more. No one was here. None of it made sense. Astrid laughed, head thrown back, with the moon high above Toyen Pool, shining on fjord, city, and mountain.

She jumped in, and cold blue water engulfed her, swirled around her, entered each pore and probed each entry into her form. She twirled in the water, swam down to the light globe, and glided like an elf through the silver blue lights. She opened and closed her eyes in the water, silver membranes shielding her pupils. She flexed her hands, felt the webbing between the finger joints, and felt the speed. Cartwheel, duck weave, eel ride.

ANDREW SZILVASY

SNAKE LIPS

Under the lone stone, the eel
hid from the white light.
Tempted, maybe, by the fiddler
crab, body-
sized orange claw held out like

Hector when outside
the walls he begged for life. The eel
sat quiet, no
pitched fight or fast strike for our
eyes. But floating scraps

the morning after gave such joy
to boys still
eager for some war. Better
yet, the albino
red snake down the block with pink eyes

and orange
skin was ready to be fed.
This white mouse had eyes
pink as the snake's, but mammal sight
could not help

it up the glass. All pets are
imposters: the orange
tabby that purrs in your pink lap,
eyes a dis-
tant bird, and pierces your leg.

SONJA JOHANSON

OSAGE ORANGES AT THE ARNOLD

A garden, yes, but also
a haven for lovers,
addicts, joggers
and other lost souls
choking to death
on the city

A tree museum
where we are curating
species we are wiping out
beside species we are bringing in
that kill

Forbidden, yes
but not the fruit of knowledge
only a hedge apple
long divorced
from its seed disperser, whispering
where are the mammoths? and
how did I get here?

Snakes, torpid now,
even the images
carved into this skin
a frieze full of miniscule elvers,
a green brain moving,
heavy in the hand –
the weighty sin
of stealing them

KIRK WESTPHAL

HOW I WILL ESCAPE

All the day's unspoken thoughts
mill and fester about
until they notice me,
slinking toward a door
I suppose might be there.
They press in,
eager for an audience,
crooked and agape.

I hear the woman who tried to seduce me
selling herself to all my friends.

I see a thousand dollars in an open box
but a painter hands it to a priest.

Beside me is the woman I imagined kissing
but she is snake-eyed, covered in chain mail.

I murmur I'll try again tomorrow.

In the corner I see Jesus Christ
spitting back my name.

ALAINA PEPIN

I BEND MY MOUTH ON TRUTH

In December I set my kitchen table on fire
and buff my skin with ash and chips of paint
that were left behind. I lick pickle juice

from a blue willow plate and crack the china
in half. Maybe if I bathe my palms in salt
and aloe and blood, the stink of sulfur

and Castrol will lose its bite. I'm tired
of apologies, the way my mouth bends
to form the words. Once, in a coffee

shop across from a bar, an old man
told me the key to a happy life is to
live well, to pay taxes, to not be afraid

to tell a lie here and there. But I wonder
what would happen if I told the truth,
if I stopped chewing back the way

my heart blooms on my tongue like
carnations, full and red and open.
I don't remember when I first understood

how Saint Peter felt, when it became so
easy to deceive. I think when the sirens
come, I'll show the cops my sooty palms.

KRIS KUNZ

WHAT YOU CAN

In the morning I choose the perfect color. Some days I love olive, some days, not. This is important because I know I won't have a say in my burial outfit. Someone will decide black leather isn't appropriate, or a silver puffer looks too much like a space-suit in a coffin, so I can't worry about that. But I can pick what I'll be found in. You have to make the decisions you can. I used to carry copies of my book in the car, carpooled them around like bundled children, until I realized there was no place to drop them off. No one was waiting for them to burst through a door, take off their coats, stay awhile. I bought a white wool coat because a snowy owl whispered *om* before she left me with no luck, a little bourbon and a horseshoe-shaped hole, which was also the shape of my high school. Since then, everyone leaks out the open end and I'm stuck with the stains — grass, lipstick, rings on the nightstand and saliva-dabbed smudges of wine and blood — which so ruin a snow-white coat, which otherwise would be perfect to wear on a dying day, or any other day I can imagine they'd find me.

ADAM SCHEFFLER

SLEEPING BEAUTY

We got it wrong – the prince's kiss puts her
to sleep as, for decades, he and his friends
watch football farting, pelting
the TV with a hail of Cheetos whose
orange poison pollen she scrubs later
on hands and knees from the carpet, a
dreaminess steeling across her eyes
green as thorns, green as the walls where
she sleepwalks from room to room
keeping up the spell of sameness —
mop and broom, tuck and iron – and only
when he chews steak, retells the story
of how he kicked the 'dumbass teacher's
dog down the road,' does she say
'that's horrible' before — her eyes fluttering
like a doll's — she slips back down
into the stream of her living sleep, waves
lapping at her like a white dress, tiny
version of herself screaming in her
ear — and things carry on in just this way
until one night after scrubbing and cooking
for hours she sees, on the local news,
a dead prostitute's face grinning like
a scooped out pumpkin, and following some
impulse, brings hypnotized lips to the screen,
kisses the woman's pixellated white brow,
and when the prince next pinches her ass
& leans in for the kiss, she slaps him,
packs her bags and leaves, truck peeling
out down the dirt road from the castle,
windows jammed down, pulse singing at
her finger-tips, and they find him stroke-dead
in front of the TV six months later in the
now dirt-caked house, limbs bloated,
eyes pecked out by their pet parrot,
and all the coroners agree that they've
never seen such an ugly corpse.

DIZ WARNER

MICHIGAN SILK

Childhood walks in a Michigan field introduced me to my first
human corpses.

Most days, I whiffled sideways through the dense evergreen
border of my family's lawn. The tatted hands of the arborvitae
slapped against my play-clothes, except in winter when the
snow-heavy limbs landed more like a sock. But this was summer.
I often paused between the tall wavy trees, holding their frond-
like needles to my face. They produced seeds on their sunny side
and smelled like newly woven baskets. Sometimes I shot between
their lacy arms into the tangled field on the other side, catching
my pants on briars that left tiny red scratches beneath the fabric.

The border was planted for my family's privacy but gave me
mine as I disappeared, or so I fancied, into scratchy high bush,
goldenrod, Indian grass, and a stand here and there of black
walnut, maple, chokecherry, hickory, and spruce, little islands
of trees surrounded by a messy Michigan wildflower salad that
attracted pheasants, quail, goldfinches, meadowlarks, grackles,
box turtles, woodchucks, and the black-capped chickadees, the
first bird I learned. It remains my idea of simple charm--its black
cap and bib, white cheeks and fluffy underbelly, buffy sides with
bits of gray, and easy fearlessness.

At the western edge of my field, wetland plants exploded in a
small fen. Cattail and milkweed grew in luxurious abundance.
tMy big sister had been in a play in Detroit with the horror film
actor Vincent Price. One of his lines about will-o'-the-wisps
sailing lazily above a bog, brighter than the moonlight, stuck
with me and I half-expected to turn and see flashing sprites dart
around my shoulders. In autumn, like any other kid, I chased
after floss escaping from milkweed pods but stopped before
grabbing it off the breeze. The silky fibers drop seed to take root
in new ground. It was hard not to touch something so fragile, so
soft. But if I wasn't greedy, they might shine their ghost lights
elsewhere.

As with the chickadees, I have a lasting loyalty to milkweed.
Right now I have a bowl of pods on my desk. They have split
open and slowly the silk is distributing itself around the room.
American colonists once used the silk for pillow stuffing.

In the 1940s, it held commercial promise as mattress filling and insulation. Thomas Edison unsuccessfully tried to turn the plant into rubber, as did World War II Scientists. It was used in the war to stuff life preservers. Now it is primarily the focus of conservation efforts for the critical role it plays in the life of the monarch butterfly, which favors the leaf bottoms as a hideaway for its green and gold chrysalis. The pods I have were plucked by a friend from a vacant lot that was tarred over, but the milkweed found a crack, found a way.

My field was busied by history and felt ancient to me. Before European settlers drove the Native Americans west, Potawatomi probably hunted where I played. Quail skimmed by, holding their cinnamon plumes high. Rabbits watched from the understory for a split second then vanished. The ring-necked pheasant I regularly spooked would have made a good chicken-sized meal, but fast, and hard to nail with a bow and arrow. My pheasants seemed to evolve knowing I ate frozen TV dinners with Fanny Mae on Saturday nights, and the aluminum trays didn't include their iridescent green and white-banded necks. The birds would flap upwards in a squawking panic, only to alight a short distance further and strut ahead, their long coppery tails, with thin, black arrowhead markings, pertly sticking out behind them. The great spirits may have intended the creatures and plants of my field as meals for hunter-gatherers, but me, I just wanted to hug them.

Usually I would explore a section of the field with a beach bucket and scoop, sandwich bags for collecting, and a scratched magnifying glass. Fanny Mae, who looked nearly as old as the Potawatomi, said I spent more time out there than a katydid. Together we tipped my tadpoles specimens into a cleaning pal to grow them up frogs. Within days, we buried them beneath lilac bushes in the garden. A few sprouted nascent legs before dying.

What I failed to realize is that anyone could see me just fine. I wasn't hidden at all. Our next door neighbors, the Golden's, had a fence around their pool low enough that anyone standing up could see me rummaging around out back. Fanny often watched me from her room on our second floor. Fanny was different. She loved everything I did. Pussywillows, chipping sparrows, the rabbits. She found a universe in them as I did. She would join me to watch squirrels patching their nests with mouthfuls of leaves, walking sticks carefully twinning a thin bramble, or at a fat worm wriggling into the loam.

Beyond the Golden's fenced-in pool was a bank of harried-looking shrubs and sticker plants. There the soil turned sandy. The vegetation offered resistance to the wind that sifted through the branches or swept above and over the natural hedgerow. I dug out a huge hole and called it a fort. I rolled a fallen bough in for a seat and made steps and shelves from rocks, storing my collecting things there. A few feet away on the unsheltered side of the fort, the field abutted another fence with a gate, hinged open. One day I squirmed right through and found myself on the long, manicured and ornamental lawn alongside the processional driveway to Ira Kaufman's Funeral Home. The sprinklers clicked away on the opposite side.

I was trespassing! I was overwhelmed with guilt, thrilled by the danger, but apparently safe. The lawn was empty. I walked around to the side of the building, turning my head like an owl, eyeing the grounds for a fast-approaching, disapproving adult. An unspectacular door was ajar, similar to the door to my school's small auditorium. I stepped inside. It was dark and cave-like, with light winking through a stained glass window above a dais. My eyes adjusted to empty velvety pews and rays of color fanning out across the room. A white head parted the rainbow, glowing like the moon. It was a person, an old woman sleeping with her hands folded below a long strand of pearls. The pearls formed a U on her chest, the rest covered at the nape by her flossy white hair. She was cradled in satin and gleaming wood. I waited for the being to emerge that was crouched inside her stillness. Dust motes sifted through layers of hue, stippling along the surface of her gown. Her eyes threatened to open and spill skeins of silk all the way to my feet. I watched but her eyelids never once fluttered. The longer I watched, the more they seemed to lay like sheets over a davenport in a home closed up for summer.

I understood then and fled out the door, through newly awakened sprinklers. My wet shoes, socks and clothes gathered bits of bark, burrs, leaf and dirt as I picked up speed, breaking through the arborvitae with my very first serious crime thumping in my blood like The Super Chicken Theme Song.

When you find yourself in danger,
When you're threatened by a stranger,
When it looks like you will take a lickin'
Just Call for Super Chicken!
Cluck, cluck, cluck!

I had seen a dead person. I went back again as soon as I could.

An old man dressed for the Fisher Theater, but wearing a yarmulke, was laid out. His skin too had sheen, but he seemed deader than the old woman had and I was disappointed that it wasn't her, as if she and I had shared an intimacy, as if she might have become a great-aunt. Would there always be someone new? Someone who wasn't all there?

Another man stepped out from behind a long burgundy curtain. He was not shiny like the man lying down but he was hornet-mad. He chased after me scolding, caught me, demanded my name, and told my mother, who rightly wondered aloud why Ira Kaufman left its chapel door open in the first place.

I knew I wasn't going to be punished. No one wanted to think about what kind of child would visit dead strangers, and as my uncle said, it wasn't like I'd robbed the place. I'd left the pearl necklace alone, though the milky strand drifted after me through time.

Those bodies, in couture as fancy as Hudson Department Store mannequins, blinked on and off in my head like fireflies for a long time and I can still see them as if I were having tea and they flop in wing chairs on either side of me.

Land developers bought my field eventually and filled in the fen. I went back once in adulthood and the field seemed so small, a postage stamp, now with a few close-together houses and grass rolled out on top of it.

Today, the sky tapped out rain from morning to dusk. Cardinals, doves, and sparrows made a Roman Bath of a puddle in my yard, where a rabbit keeps her den. Squirrels chase in the day and the skunks, with their funny skittering ramble, emerge at night. Chickadees dip by on their small wings I still curb squeals of delight in order not to frighten them away. Living my life I have forgotten and remembered constant death, and forgotten again, even after it thieved loved ones and shorn me to my core.

Somewhere milkweed is pushing up where least expected, and will again.

KAREN PAUL HOLMES

THE L-SHAPED HOUSE, PACKARD AVENUE, FLINT, MICHIGAN

I grew up on *Do the Watusi* on the jukebox at Angelo's,
pink tutus,
and a bike looping along
sidewalk and driveway—I was Andretti
but obeyed stop signs my brother chalked
on the pavement.
My Barbie wore homemade dresses,
and boys picked me because I could bat.

There was the Easter hat, carnation corsage,
and communion
on an empty stomach, wine digging a hot path—
throat to belly, while we sang, *Mnogaya Leta!*
God grant us many years!

My breath is Klashoff and Papazoff with rags
for shoes in winters beneath Baba Mountain.
Bortkevitch and Ryan, Russian ships
and Newcastle's bagpipes on Saturdays,

a tailor's even stitches, a prudish mother's fear
of disgrace (we necked with boys anyway),
the expectation of all-As at Bentley High
and anxiety. The family cracked up
at Carol Burnett on Sunday nights
or inside jokes like calling me
Chef Girl-R-D.

Our house hid a half-acre backyard
with a rusty red swing set, woods running
way back to the train track.
We weren't supposed to play there but waved
to cabooses and left
pennies for engines to flatten.

I sweat Baltic and Pacific salt, the sweet grit
of Great Lakes sand, the popping bite of chili dogs.
Fortunes and misfortunes have intermingled—
a lamb manga simmered all day.
Moments quiver, semi-opaque
like fruit-dotted Jell-O,
      or wink like candles counting years
on the glossy frosting of devil's food cake.

CJ GIROUX

BASELINE

My daughter clatters down the carpeted stairs, too fast, too loud. Her arms out, she skips the last step to alight on the uneven planks of our dining room. She stumbles, teeters on her heels. She's worried about tonight's band performance at St. Mary's cathedral, schoolmates' reaction to her outfit. With fingers splayed, she sinks towards the floor and then moves back and forth on the balls of her feet, crouching like a runner preparing to steal second.

I want to tell Grace to go ahead, to run with abandon, to fly like a sparrow that knows its destination and not worry about the consequences, but I know better about consequences, her temperament, mine, and as she rights herself, I'm the one who feels off-balance; unable to speak, I catch a whiff of freshly-mown grass though the open window and return to my childhood, summer nights defined by Red Rover, freeze-tag, frisbees.

The infield for our nightly kickball game was the only treeless yard on the block, though its owners, our next-door neighbors, had no kids young or old enough to play. Home plate was the corner of our lot where yard met house, where hostas brokered the border between grass, bush, the splash of green on white spreading like a rash. We barreled down the sloping driveway to first base and then along the sidewalk to the Russells' drive; third was a stand of forsythia bushes that pushed forth only leaves, and our house, home. Our paths were invisible, but the right angle from second to home was etched on the Bundys' lawn like lines on a treasure map leading to an empty X. The thwack of ball on Keds and Converses ended only when streetlights became suns. We moved, breathless, with sureness, certainty, sweat.

On this night though, I am once again sidelined, penned to the porch, relegated to sitting with my youngest siblings. Bathed for bed, they suck on popsicles, orange stains growing into the over-exaggerated smiles of clowns. They wear shorty pajamas, too small, mismatched, covered in polka dots, Calamine. This is more circus finery. I am next to, slightly behind my mother, her hair still black, who watches the game from her patio chair, sinks into its ribbing. The dog, its tight apricot curls, pants under this aluminum throne, leash wrapped around my mother's hand. I want to watch the game, but don't want to be seen by my friends. I squat, balance on my toes, peer over the bushes so flat, so even it looks as if my father uses a level when he trims them.

Danny releases the ball. It spins toward my brother and bounces once before it sinks below my sightline. I never see Steve connect, a pop up to the pitcher's mound. "Out," Mom snaps, ump, arbitrator, league president. She is always right, rules with wooden spoons, soap—over All, Dawn, Tide, Joy.

Third out, the teams switch, and Steve zigzags to left field. He crouches, moves side to side on his toes. I do the same, my feet all pins and needles. Randy tenses for the pitch. I want to stand up, lean closer to the action, but I don't need to advertise to my friends that I've received a one-game suspension. They know, I know they know, but still to advertise it… so I just mentally cheer for Angela, the only girl our age on the block, and shut my eyes. I count to ten, look to her success, and lean into the whitewashed door, hair catching on the screen. I stare above, study the bronze eagle, wings outstretched, screwed above the door's frame, into mortar.

"You," Mom says, pointing at me with her nail file. I have been caught swearing. Washed with Lux, I burn inside and out. The wax of soap clings to the back of my tongue; bile climbs the throat, retreats, returns. She intones the warning that is mine and mine only: "You are the oldest. You have a duty." Her voice is calm, lacks anger, but I know better than to roll my eyes. Instead I follow the grackle that bisects the heat hovering over the asphalt outfield. The bird homes towards its nest.

In my more generous moods, when I remember this night, these moments, I freeze the bird midair—the ball hangs, haloed, like a host dipped in altar wine—and I know my mother was trying to say, you can be better; you aren't there yet, but will be. Perhaps she was really punishing her flaws. What I heard, though, was you're wrong, off, less; you are not enough. And so, for a while anyway, I learned to keep quiet, to swear under my breath, to divorce outer from inner and pretend to accept, get along, play the role. Duty, however, was just another four-letter word. Like Mom's Goddammits, Jesus Christs, and that holy trinity of shit-shit-shit, duty carried heat like an infected bug bite, bleeding at the edges.

My sister will believe this story even if she doesn't recall it. My mother probably won't remember it and then will worry, at least momentarily. My father will support my mother. My brothers could be split, on opposite teams, the kickball still hanging above, between them; they could, depending on the day, both be eager to catch it, both racing to get there first.

Today though, I let that maroon ball of my childhood clear the yellow hood of a neighbor boy's rusting Torino forever parked in our street, stalled. And when this red sphere slices through the air, I return to the present, to see Grace standing tall, straightening her glasses, smoothing her dress—covered in ragged circles of maroon, pink, white, midnight blue and bought at Target with money she's saved. The hem hits her knee, hovers over boots with horizontal buckles that ladder up her legs. She asks how she looks.

"Beautiful," I say. She rolls her eyes and won't smile, but she blushes. For once, she believes me.

I know though that this moment, this comment, is probably not the truth Grace will recall. Instead, this conversation, her childhood, will arc like a four-square ball bouncing out of bounds, or a red-winged blackbird passing her vision, his epaulets a flash of yellow-orange light. Because I remember the way I do, and my siblings the way that they do, I worry about what she will choose to remember, as if what we remember is chosen. And since she is an only child, who will challenge her version of events? I worry her focus will only be on fear, judgment, failings, those she attaches to her herself, classmates, me. I worry she will remember crows, their blue-black caws speaking with my voice—start acting your age; stop acting your age; stop worrying about what others think, did you just say what I think you said? These birds, I fear, will bleat constant queries about homework, chores, musical scales. You know better, they will say. You have a duty. There are, they will squawk, consequences.

However, if I'm lucky, some days these crows will be silenced, and balls will hover between baselines and boundaries like airy notes rising from her flute. In those moments, on those days, I pray that I will have been enough for her. That most of her memories will glow like maroon spheres of light, red balloons rising. That most of her memories will burn with the sureness of a fast pitch accurately delivered, turn like the shift from a sharp to a flat, rise with the joy of a red-tailed hawk at dusk wheeling on summer currents before homing back to its nest.

BRENDAN SHERRY

PRATT AND ASHLAND

To what degree
were their minds raised
outside the tackle
of royalty

and how did the riddle go
that a dog could not put
a deep enough hole
in the earth
so he apologized into it

and then reeds grew
out of the hole
and they whispered
to everybody

these casual
tossed-off apologies
with teeth
you needed gloves
to dispose of

HEART OF ALENE

There is no drawing
tonight and tomorrow
about the scene of the gap

no road after
clearing the border

only houses
oysters
and overcast

there was a minute
you did not want
the world to be at rest

but considered all of it
as the continuation
of a heartbeat

the success of white
and gray stone
over the pall of water

the sequences over which
heaven must lock
in order to equip
itself with a place
between gunpoint
and call

LOVE IS LIKE A ROCK

She closed the book and placed it on the table. As she stepped into the den, she said to her husband, "Someone else has gone and written *my* novel."

He sat on the couch, his head tilted back, their baby daughter asleep in his arms. The television was on, an old British science-fiction show they'd bought on DVD and watched between his shifts as an E.R. resident a few years ago, before the baby, before life got hard from the inside.

When she saw the thin rubber tourniquet around her husband's arm, her eyes stung with anger. He hadn't promised never again, but he had promised never again with the baby right there.

She picked up the child without waking her and took her upstairs. When she returned, she walked up to her husband and smacked him as hard as she could across the face, ptartly to show her anger, partly to wake him. His body slumped to the side. She slapped him again in panic. She looked at her hand. All the stinging—her eyes, her hand—stopped.

After the funeral, people gathered at his parents' house. His old college friends talked about the stranglehold of addiction. She nodded but knew that explained only part of anything. Her husband had medicated himself and made a mistake. Rehab didn't work well for physicians. They'd moved to a new town that had ridden the booms and busts of mining for a hundred years and kept going. But he'd returned to the emergency room, negotiating with fate. "If only I'd called him," several of his friends said, as if a voice from the past would've reminded him to be someone else.

In his friends' memories, she saw glimpses of her husband. They mentioned peculiar things he said and did. They liked him all the same. *All the same,* she thought, nodding. One woman recounted, "He came to my mom's house one weekend to decorate her tree. While we were sorting ornaments and untangling hooks, he hung saltine crackers on the tree. My mom left them up. Who's to say what belongs?"

Later that night, when it was just family sitting around, her sister-in-law said she'd recently read a marvelous novel. "Have you read it?" she asked.

It was the one she'd been finishing when her husband put a needle into his vein and left her.

Listening to the din of voices, she thought of her husband's favorite song, the one his college friends had mentioned. Her husband had made people wonder whether he was serious. *Love really is like a rock*, she thought, hearing the song in her head. Hard and heavy, with something sharp and bright running through its core. Looking across the room, watching family members pass her baby from person to person, she knew she couldn't depend on anyone but, nonetheless, had to rely on everyone.

"I've read that book," she said. "When I finished, I adored it for five minutes."

UNBREAKABLE

It's the handwriting on the envelope that catches my attention, because it's mine.

I'd been hoping for a letter from you, or maybe trying not to hope. I didn't know when — if — you'd write back, and I've written you so many letters that never reached an end, let alone the mailbox, that not-hoping just became another reason to stack the mail unread on the table near the door. As if I needed another reason not to look.

But there it was, waiting for me: a personal letter, three sheets folded inside a thick, cream envelope with your name written on it in my own block letters. It had come back to me with something added, a stamp of faded blue ink that obscured the first letters of your name: "Return to Sender: Attempted — Not Known."

I last saw you by accident. It was — I have to pause to think — nearly twenty years ago. It was some philanthropic event, something social that filled a medium-sized room. I don't remember the cause, only that I wanted to be seen to support it; appearances still mattered to me then. I'd stayed as long as I thought I needed and turned to shake one last hand, and there you were. You were looking at me looking at you. I could tell you were surprised, but maybe you were also delighted. I waited until you took a step toward me. My legs felt unsteady, but I met you in the middle.

You'd changed, in some way I couldn't define. It was as if I thought I knew a secret about you, but now everybody could see it. All I knew for certain was that I had never seen any woman more beautiful than you were at that moment, in that room.

I said it was good to see you, which was as close as I'd come that night to saying what I meant. You said you were just visiting the city. You were married, which I knew, and had two small children, which I did not.

"No children for me," I said.

Your smile barely curved your mouth at the corners; your right eyebrow rose in that almost undetectable way. "I'm not surprised," you said. The old challenge.

I started to rise to it, but you looked away to rummage in your handbag and then you were showing me photos of your children — two girls. "They look like my husband," you said, but to me they looked just like you.

And we made small talk — the smallest of small talk, the *who what when where*; never the *why*. In these small things, I had nowhere to place a foot and feel the ground common between us. It was inconceivable, this soft, banal conversation, when for half a decade you'd been the most important thing in my life. Back then we'd been all furious boil and killing frost; I didn't know what to do with this tepid water in between.

And then you looked at your watch and said, apologetically, that you had to go. A hundred thoughts came to me, but I have often been caught in that place that comes between the thing and the words. I have never been able to say what I mean.

"I—" I began, and when I hesitated your eyes seemed to stop blinking, just for a moment, until I repeated, "It was good to see you," which was no longer what I meant to say.

I could see some thought cross your face, but instead of speaking you leaned forward, your head turned carefully to the side. We hugged with the distant politeness of one-time acquaintances.

And I fled, walking directly toward the exit. I tried not to hurry, but when someone began to turn toward me, his mouth opening, I tapped my wristwatch as if the time mattered and I kept walking.

But just past the doorway I stopped. I should go back, I thought. I should tell you how happy I am to hear about your life — about this rich, full, wonderful life of yours that is not also mine. If I could hear myself saying it, maybe I could believe it to be true. I came back into the room and looked for you, but you weren't there. You'd said you had to go; you'd gone.

I hold the letter to you in my hand and sigh, an exhale of disappointment and a little annoyance. Of course the address is outdated. You've moved; that's what people do. I've lost most of my ties to that part of my life — or dropped them, really, not on purpose but also not by accident. I've heard news about you every now and again, from friends of friends, in small, disconnected bits that come without warning or context. I know the threads connecting us have grown frayed, but any strong cable has so many woven strands that it can lose a few without losing its strength. I know I can find you.

Still, I can't put the letter down. I'd expected an answer or a not-answer, not this thing in between. That "Now Known" unsettles me.

It's somehow fitting that it's Chris who calls me. After all, so many roads lead to Chris. When I became your boyfriend he was your ex — but instead of going away, there he was with his own new, very nice girlfriend, always friendly, always there. It drove me mad sometimes that I could find no purchase for my anger, no ally in my awkwardness. I resented Chris — and admired him, too, which burned my resentment deeper. That's why I didn't want to call him about you, even though I knew Chris always stays in touch with everybody, and in fact I didn't call him. But Chris is always there, and somehow now he is calling me.

"I didn't know you hadn't heard," he says. Even over the attenuation of the telephone line, his voice is deep, even deeper than I remember. Maybe it's the weight — of responsibility, of time — or maybe it's the gravity that comes from being a judge, as he's been for many years. Probably he now calls himself Christopher, but he doesn't correct me. *After all*, he would probably say, *the two of us go way back.*

"No," I say. "I guess I've been out of touch."

"Yes," he says, but there is no accusation in his tone. I expect him to continue but instead there's a pause that makes the breath catch in my chest. Finally he says, "I'm sorry to have to tell you," and then he pauses again, this time to clear his throat. It sounds to me like rustling sand. "You see … she passed away, the summer before last."

"Oh," I say. "Ah." My mind has gone blank.

"Cancer," he adds, answering the question I haven't asked. He must be pressing his mouth against the phone; I can hear him breathing. "I'm sorry to say it wasn't quick."

Our words blur after that, but there aren't too many. I don't ask about your funeral. It won't surprise you that he's kind to me, which he doesn't have to be. He knows as well as me, I think, that this is the last time we will speak.

After I set the phone down I feel the stillness of the late

afternoon — the motionless leaves wilting beneath the sun, the road in front of the house absent the hiss and hum of passing cars. The stillness was already here; what's new is that now I notice it. The world hasn't changed at all, really, but it feels like change. You've been gone for more than two years; why hadn't I felt the world shift beneath me?

Because I did feel the world shift when we broke up for that last time. I'd come to meet you for a fight, or for a reconciliation, and probably for both. That was the rhythm I knew, the back and forth, hot and cold — the constant motion I thought was the same thing as going somewhere. You were quiet when I found you, looking dark-eyed into the middle distance, but when I sat down on the opposite end of the bench, you looked at me. I didn't see the ferocity I'd expected to see. I expected passion; what I saw was closer to compassion, or maybe to sorrow. Your eyes were as black and unblinking as the lens of that bulky camera you carried on our hikes. It felt like a long time, but it had only been a few weeks since we'd gone to your favorite part of that long trail. Because I was tromping dully on the path, my eyes on my own feet, the flap of the crane's wings caught me by surprise. But you already had the camera up to your face. I could hear the shutter snap once, then twice more in slow syncopation. After the bird's languid flight had taken it beyond the distant line of trees you said to me, *You need to catch things when you can.*

Something rattled. Metal, coming from your hand, which you'd clenched into a fist on your knee. When you opened that fist there was the ring with two keys — building, apartment — and the charm shaped like the paw of our cat. The paw was pinkish gold and covered in nicks and scratches.

"You're going?" I said. My voice sounded flat, more like a statement than a question, which was not the way I felt.

"I've already moved my things," you said. How could that be true? The keys were hanging from your fingers, swinging from the metal paw. We didn't have a cat, not anymore; we'd buried his ashes in the city park where you'd found him, shrunken and thin, hiding behind the shrubbery. He hadn't lived long enough to make the move to this apartment, but you'd kept the keyring.

I let the keys dangle from your fingers. "How?" I said, although that was not the question I had in my mind.

Something painful crossed your face, but only for a moment. You looked down and put the keys onto the bench between us.

I could see the strokes of the brush that had coated the wood slats with thick green paint. "I left a check on the hall table," you said. "For June."

I didn't know what was happening, outside or in, and no words came to me right away. In that pause your hand rose and came toward my face; I could see the fine hairs on the back of your hand, and I could almost smell the lotion you used, the one you said had no scent but always smelled to me a little like cherry cough drops.

"What about July?" I said.

Your hand stopped and your face moved sideways as if I'd slapped you. I wanted to reach out and stuff the words back into my mouth — to do *something* — but my hands and arms and chest were numb and massive and would not move. You looked down and ran your hands over the thighs of your jeans, back and forth, back and forth.

"Okay," you said, still looking down, and then you stood up with a speed that startled me. When you walked away I expected you to turn back so that everything could be alright again, but you didn't, and when I finally reached over to those abandoned keys, to touch my fingers to where you'd been sitting, the wood was already cold.

I expected something to happen next, because that's the way our story had to work: the rising action, the obstacles overcome, this darkest hour — and then the crisis and the triumph, and the glimpse of the new world ever after. But I'd misunderstood the arc; the ending had already come. Everything that has a beginning must have an ending, but sometimes, up close, everything looks like everything else. Sometimes it's only afterward that we can see the shape.

So it's only now that I understand: That afternoon was the penultimate time. I used to love the grandeur of that word, *penultimate*. When I first came across it as that bookish, quiet kid reading in the corner, I thought it must mean something like *extra-ordinary*, that it must mean super-ultimate. But what I took for majesty was just a word that means *next to last*. For all its grandness, the penultimate is something you know only when you know the ultimate. You know the next-to-last only when you know the last.

There are things about you — about me and you — that I remember, and things about myself I know I've forgotten, but

I've always known that you could help me piece them together. When we were together I relied upon you to remember where we'd gone for Christmas the year before, when we'd last seen my friends, that thing my mother wanted me to remember, and I've relied upon your memory since. You know things nobody else knows, so our pieces, together, could make a whole. This life I call mine is scattered among a hundred people, and sometimes I wonder if I have enough pieces of my own to make the picture whole. Even if I forgot — when I forgot — you could remember for me. Someday I would figure out how to ask.

They say that if the sun went dark, the darkness wouldn't reach us for more than eight minutes. For 500 seconds we would look to the sunlight and think it would last forever. Is it the darkness that would reach us, or the light that would depart? Is light the absence of darkness or darkness the absence of light? *The light shineth in darkness,* they read to me in Sunday school, *and the darkness comprehended it not.* That's also where they taught me that *apocalypse* means the same thing as *t*; what makes us shiver is not the end, but the knowledge of the end.

I thought the silence between us was a tangible thing, not the emptiness of the void but an invisible aether: Even if only we could sense it, this quintessence would connect us always. I thought that silence was a thing that could always be broken.

When I held the envelope to my lips and sealed it with my tongue, I didn't know that the silence was already unbreakable.

CATHERINE ANDERSON

ILLUSION

Weeks after my husband died, I traveled
Hallow's Eve into the dark cyclone

of the city where I passed through the knotted
silk of traffic at rush hour,

then drifted along the avenue with a bramble
of sheeted ghosts and witches

until my friend—her face smiling,
mica-bright—waved me down as the last

coins of daylight dropped to earth.
In that quick shuffle, I marked

how the present envelopes the past
like an accordion of mirrors,

my husband already twenty-five days
through his *bardo*, and still not there,

not home to the other side.
At the restaurant, the waiter, his head

and arms wrapped like a mummy,
took our order of bun with anchovy sauce,

leaned down to hear our voices through
the white gauze. I forgot it was Halloween,

assumed the young man was severely burned,
his injury a public stillness held inside

while the room brimmed with sorrow then
kindness, an illusion I kept to myself

as he carried water from table to table,
laid out the spring rolls with basil.

R. THOMAS SHEARDY

A WOMAN LIKE NOVEMBER

November abhors colors: especially greens.
I knew a woman like that once.

She hated green: any viridian, every *terre verte*.
(She was a painter and she knew all her colors by name:
        oxide of chromium and *phthalocyanine*)

How bright and sunny she was when she arrived,
As if the summer had got itself caught in her hair
And then followed her about like a Flemish halo
        Or Guadalupe's *mandorla*.

And then, like November, one by one, she began to blow her colors away.
"I don't like this one, today," she'd say, and, "I hate this one too…"
She'd scrape them off and fling them aside.
She stopped cleaning her brushes.
They grew stiff and brittle from neglect.
Her pigments hardened and cracked like lichens on November tree
        trunks.

My palette seemed bright then, but lonely.
        Lying by itself on the taboret.

When black and white December arrived,
A beautiful limner with chalks and charcoal,
        The painter left.

December suited me then.
        Her flat etchings and hard-edged monoprints purified my palette.

Together, we now render our lives in shades of gray,
As shadows cast by colorless trees:
        A grisaille of forgotten desires.

ED HACK

WHAT TREES DO

Clear sky. The breeze lifts up the tree's green skirts
flirtatiously. So far as I can tell,
the tree does not object nor seem averse
to play Bo Peep, enjoys the breeze's swell
between its branches and its trunk. The tree
does not reveal a thing, though one could cite
its *en masse* quivering, its banshee sprees
of craziness when storms exhaust their might
and shake it to its tangled roots that clutch
with knotted strength the buried dark of earth.
What does the tree exist to do but touch,
be touched, its life a constant state of birth
and growth and death and birth, alive with leaves
that love the winds that do just what they please.

D.R. JAMES

WHICH I DID.

Last night's
legit

big-lake horizon
looked phony-

perfect
for a musical, for

a song-and-dance
cast against

a two-tone
cutout. Then the wind

blew its
incessancy;

the surf
must've sanded

sandbars
to nubbins.

And above it all
I slept soundly —

via *un cabernet* —
and acted out

the better part
of a howling

dream-set, as if
I'd survive and

live
to see morning,

D.R. JAMES

WIRED

—after Jack Myers

What was I thinking
when, without qualifications,
except for being as cold
as anyone all last season,
I ran to get elected
County Commissioner of Winter Heat?

I was thinking of warmth,
of course, the irony involved
in commanding the motion of electrons
within a fifty-mile radius of my
two-fold ignorance: geometry
and electrical engineering.

And what was I thinking
when I yearned to prefer
the official wire required
for the job rather than
the under-the-table imitation
available for a little gift of graft?

I was thinking of the Second Coming,
of course, that seek-and-ye-shall-find
system of irrevocability, how
I would want a seat up front.

What I wanted was
inclusion, to be connected,
wired if you will,
to the universe of painlessness
unavailable to those in pain,
by which I mean everyone.

And if I gained favor
by following the ritual
of water-into-wire
then you could count me in,
count me among the sheep,
not those goats also spoken of.

What I didn't want was what Mugsy
got: jolts at inexact intervals
from an on-going present eternally
separating him from any wire at all.

D.R. JAMES

NOTEBOOK FLURRIES

It's snowing sideways, flakes
like atoms with no place to go,
papery petals that parallel
the gusty earth. Always the guest,

I have always a question, a dream
welling upside down from
the veiled sheet of stars: it's wild,
I know, but the answer hasn't

been to praise it like you would
a lean train of coyotes loping
across the road, or daffodils
if they could grow by moonlight,

thumbing their frilly noses
at the centuries of human
sacrifice and bloody cargo, or
stones cracking in the absence

and failure of trees to fashion
language from water and light.
No, it's the old song's old story:
the farmer in his field, the family

at their morning table, the spider
plucking her eight steps to the kill.
Wood, dirt, blanket, leaf, even
thighs—even eyebrows over open

lashes that fan the face that bars
the door that says goodbye. Now
only flecks that nevertheless
fly like phrases, the snow joins

the ground around the house,
all the little letters piling like books,
vowels like birdsong marking
this digression into early spring.

ANNA BERNSTEIN

IN A PARKING LOT IN NEW JERSEY,

I give my mother a small piece of news:
I can't methylate folic acid. Not at all.
The words feel good in my mouth.
I don't know why. Methylate. She loves me.
She sits into the cold leather like a bird
fluffing down in a nest. "You know," she says,
"Folic acid is important for babies." I know.
I can take pills for this. My body will
right itself, grateful for the gift, and someday
I will produce another good body from my own.
I fall asleep in the car, as I always do, rocked
by highways in a chair tipped back, my abdomen
rested in my laced fingers.
In some way I have been waiting
for this news, have read so many
mothers dreaming up monsters
in the pits of their bellies that
perhaps it was inevitable, perhaps
I had known and by knowing made so
that this always was my body's natural
pilgrimage. I can feel it, just on the edge
of dreaming, in that place of bad logic
one comes back from with a start—
the love felt not for what it could have been, but for
the real sullied mess of itself, never truly alive,
only rotating wicked-limbed and unknowable
in some redness vast as space,
far from my body as the moon.
I love you. You are me. We can be

sullied together. Listen to this, "We can be,"
hope shared with a knotted babe
that never was, like an invitation
to pick strawberries. A cracked
spine and a maze of a heart, the
wild twisting of a silhouette.
It shifts me in my sleep.
You wreckage, crashed ship,
what shore were you meant for?
I wrap my arms around you
to quiet the beating of your
many skins. I am here. I am here
for you. I am sorry to leave
your small life behind.

TODD MERCER

MISTER WONDERFUL, SOMEBODY'S DAD

He
had
a dime
bag of tricks,
flexible beliefs,
a fashion sense from yesteryear.
He whistled Kenny G songs, drove Pintos, voted wrong.
Yet (at least) one woman loved him,
one who had options.
Two kids knew
he hung
the
moon.

MERRIDAWN DUCKLER

THE NIGHT WOLVES OF RUSSIA

are brando-like, bandit-like
Russian bikers,
reported on the radio
but I have to cut off the idiot
driving in front of me so I miss the gist
of their complaint
concerning Ukraine, which a Russian taught me
never to call *the* Ukraine,
as if it was a border he sneered
with his remarkably wolf-like teeth, and pale skull
perfect for hanging over a fireplace.
"Never!" he shouted
in the loud bar named
after a U2 album
where, since it was impossible to sleep
but easy to drink
we spent each night;
a dump where first a guy grabbed my butt
and then a girl grabbed my butt, so I was well supported.
By now the radio show had moved on
and I lost the night wolves,
though I picture them cruising
inside the vast, block long
department store in St. Petersburg
where stone-cold women prevented me
from buying amber, a red source of infinite light,
a well of tears from the chained daughters,
a fossil of resin preserved before any country had borders,
though there was never a time before wolves.

MICHAEL BARTELT

WATCHING THE DEBATE THINKING,
"HAVE THEY READ LEAVES OF GRASS?"

For Hillary Clinton and Donald Trump

Wasn't it JFK who said
we get the kind of democracy
our humor deserves?

If not him, then some great American
who lived long ago, perhaps
even before Kennedy and public relations,
before FDA regulations were needed,
before television provided the self-
conscious ten pounds and declared
the winner the biggest schmoozer.

Let's jump in a patriotic time machine
and not fall to jingoism,
let's remove the –ism, leave ourselves
with jingo, a funny word that warrants
a different meaning.

Let's ask Walt what he thinks.
He's been lying face down in the grave
too long and wishes to look up
at the Goodyear Blimp.
He's never seen it,

and the fantasy of the night
goes something like CNN asking Walt,
"Mr. Whitman, would you like to moderate
tonight's super-debate for an audience of 100 million?"
And Walt says, "Sure thing."

But when it's about time for the candidates
to square off, he's nowhere to be found,
just lying on his back in Camden
watching the Goodyear Blimp
make its way north with bright letters
running across the starless American sky...
"...Whitman moderates...Tonight at 9 on CNN."

It's time to broadcast live to the American people,
and there's no cue for the candidates.
The vacant stage is refreshing.
The silence is nice,

as Whitman turns over
to face the democratic ground.

JONATHAN GREENHAUSE

REGGIE ORDERED A PACKAGE OF
MINIATURE PEOPLE,

then proclaimed himself king.   His tiny subjects
lauded his generosity,

swam in the Olympic-sized pool
of his bathroom sink,   threw raucous orgies beneath the sheets

of his cocktail napkins,   endured the Arctic-cold
of his air-con's open grates,

while his apartment's lights
were a slew of separate suns.   When Reggie's people slept,

they delicately snored   but never dreamt small,
his four walls now their world

just as they'd become his.
No one ever visited him,   & he was barely ever missed.

In time, he himself felt miniature   but never ventured outside:
He'd heard tales of giants

& was wary of their cruelty,
aware from firsthand experience   how easy it was

to be crushed by an irate pinkie,   his own gods lurking outside,
setting up their miniature scenery:

Reggie wasn't certain
to whom he belonged   but sensed he couldn't move freely,

his earliest memory   the opening of cardboard flaps
& the feel of gargantuan hands

from someone resembling himself,
a larger giant who, herself,   was simply a toy to a larger self.

DENNIS CUMMINGS

ARMADILLO

This life replete with the promises
of a protected journey offers little
more than the hope of a dry nest of leaves
in the dark night of the Panhandle.

Though hunkered and sheltered
against the torrent of enormous hail,
I imagined myself bruised and bleeding
as I paddled across the Rio Grande.

In the desert sun I dreamed I was
the subject of an inquest by the men
of Los Alamos. I was almost comfortable
before them, encased in my leathery

suit of leaves, my embryonic body
safe as a pharaoh in Thebes, sure
not to betray my fear of being
crushed by inanimate matter.

RINAT HAREL

BN AND THE OLD MAN

A sunny morning by the sea. Calm waves lick the sand. A long-legged bird hunts for tiny silvery fish in the shallows. A lone man wearing a suit walks down the beach, his eyes on the horizon.

"Oh, sorry," he says, nearly bumping into an old man performing a headstand. "Wait, no, it can't be." The suited man stoops to have a closer look at the upside-down face. "Yes, it is you!"

"But of course it is," says the old man. "I can only be me."

"What an honour," breathes the suited man, whom we'd call BN.

"The honour is all mine," replies the old man.

"Sir," says BN, "do you know who I am?"

"A man needs to know himself regardless of what others might think of him," the old man says.

BN nods. "True, true." He then glances around. "I'm surprised to see you on your own. Is your wife not here?"

The old man grins. "What would we do without our faithful wives?" he asks with a wink.

BN blushes, issues a hesitant smile, and turns to look at the hunting bird chasing its prey, running across the wet sand, ignoring both men. A pleasant breeze rises and he's thankful for the silence, though after a while he wonders what he should do. He knows the old man's morning routine is near holy, but excited at the rare opportunity, he's not ready to leave yet.

"Funny we meet," he finally says, his voice cheerful. "Lately, everyone has been comparing us, but they fail to see how times have changed. All world leaders live in style. Could you imagine me living in a shed in the middle of nowhere? I'd be made fun of!"

"We certainly can't have that," confirms the old man.

BN grins. "I knew you'd understand." He releases his tie a bit, saying, "It's getting hot."

"Why won't you take your shoes off and dip your feet in the water?" offers the old man.

"Yes, I think I will," says BN, does just that, then returns to the old man, and seats himself on the sand with his pants still rolled up, his socks neatly tucked inside the dress shoes.

The long-legged bird had flown away by now, and the glimmering sun keeps beaming in the pale summer sky.

"How long can you hold like this?" asks BN.

"For all eternity," answers the old man.

"Very impressive."

The old man says, "I'd think you had more important things to do than keep me company."

BN shakes his head. "I have some time before I'm expected in the office." He then adds with a deep sigh, "I haven't felt so relaxed in years."

"Nothing like the sea," agrees the old man. "It's why I used to come here each morning."

"I still can't believe I bumped into you," says BN. "So many things I want to ask you."

"Go ahead. I've got all the time in the world."

"I wish I knew beforehand, so I could better prepare. I seem to draw a blank now."

The old man smiles. "A good handstand energises the brain."

BN smiled thinly. "I carry so many responsibilities," he moaned. "Nobody but my voters has any appreciation for me. Especially my cabinet members; they just want to gang up and throw me to the dogs."

"I sure know how that feels," the old man slices out through his teeth, and BN, though surprised by the bitter tone, exclaims: "Exactly! Like you, no one but me has the backbone to fulfil the country's potential, the importance of our great nation."

Releasing his tie a bit more, he carries on, "The politicians, on both sides of the isle, don't get it, the media keeps trying to sabotage me, criticising my every move, making fun of me in every imaginable way, but luckily, this only strengthens both me and my loyal voters." His head bobs slightly as he speaks, and the pink of his baldness glimpses through the silver bluish comb-over.

The tall bird returns to fish in the shallows; it reminds him of a stilted clown.

"See this one?" he asks, pointing his chin at the bird. "He's like me, negotiating the treacherous waves to get what he wants. He's focused, unrelenting, hardworking. That's what strong leaders are made of. You were like that, and what tremendous challenges you faced!"

The old man slowly scissors his bent legs in the air, then brings them down one by one, and sits on the sand with his eyes on the sea.

"Toward the end I tried to imagine fifty years into the future," he says. "I came up with various scenarios. I suppose a nation's path is carved out by many factors, not only its leaders' strengths and capabilities."

"To be honest," says BN, looking at his companion with glimmering eyes, "I see my work as a natural continuation of yours."

The old man glimpses him. "You don't need my approval," he utters with a shake of the head, grains of sand fly out of his white hair, and BN thinks he would never have allowed his own hair to look like two fluffs of candy cotton sticking from each side of the head.

"Would you have voted for me?" he asks, wondering what flavour the old man's hair might have been, had it been made of … vanilla, he decides. French vanilla. Or maybe coconut?

The old man chortles, and BN winces, fearing his friend might have guessed his contemplations.

"Doesn't look like you need my vote, either," says the old man when his laugh subsides.

BN swallows hard. "It would be good to have it, nevertheless."

But the old man doesn't seem to be listening. His eyes linger on the far horizon, his mind drifting.

BN decides to be patient and quietly looks at the sea as well.

"I thought by now we'd have a peace agreement of some sort," the old man finally says, and BN thinks he can hear some sadness in his voice. "But that might be just an old man's sentimentality."

"We have come a long way since our early days," BN says, his doughy face clouds in thoughtfulness. "But in some ways, nothing has changed; our enemies still connive to obliterate us."

The old man nods, saying, "And still no borders …"

"Like the Americans when they got their independence," says BN with a smirk. "But sir," he carries on, and his expression turns serious, "as you correctly said long ago, *they* do not exist as a nation, and therefore the land is—always has been—ours to take."

The old man looks at BN with surprise. "I said it was ours, *all* of it?"

BN flushes, replying," Well, not exactly, but from what you have said, on *many* occasions, it would be only logical to conclude—"

"Logic, schmogic," says the old man with a dismissive wave of the hand, and rises to his feet. "You really need to try headstands; it'll help you see the world from a fresh angle."

And with that, he leans forward, and soon he is upside down again, his cotton candy hair in the wet sand.

At that moment, a small band of youngsters in bathing suits walks by, and one of them, a tall guy in orange surfing shorts, points toward the older gentlemen, calling, "Hey, look!" which startles the bird away.

The group quickly envelopes the men, yammering, "Oh, wow," and, "How cool is that?" and a tanned woman pulls out a Smartphone from her bikini bra, announcing, "Photo!"

BN, though reluctant to share his friend with strangers, is nonetheless beaming at them, proud to be found beside a historical figure of such calibre.

"Hey grandpa," asks the guy in the orange shorts, crouching beside the old man. "Could you take a picture of us with the PM?"

No reply. The old man seems to be in deep meditation.

"Oh, leave him alone," reproached a curly girl. "Can't you see he's dead?"

Alarmed, BN jumps to his feet, crying, "Don't you know who this is?" But they don't seem to have heard him, and the tanned woman gathers everyone round BN for a few selfies, then shows them to her friends, who quack and giggle, urging her to post them on social media, which she does.

BN, all the while, lectures them about the old man's epic achievements—his voice deep, brow creased—taken aback only when his palms don't meet the solid surface of the podium behind which he imagined himself standing. When he looks up he is astonished to see a hasty swarm of people approaching them. Time to leave, he muses, and starts inching away, barefoot.

"It's true," yells someone in the nearing crowd. "He is here!" And with that, the cheering throng blocks BN's escape route, and he surrenders to the hands that want to shake his, the showered hugs, more selfies. But no, he did not forget his friend, who has remained in his upturned position.

"Sir," he calls to the old man, "do I have your vote?"

"What does it matter?" replies the old man. "Like the girl said, I'm already dead."

"But would you support me?" BN's plea hovers in the air as the enthusiastic band of fans carries him away. He tries to break free, but the strong youngsters hold him tight, his protest drowned by their calls, "Long live the king, long live the king!"

The long-legged bird returns to the beach after the mob has vanished. The old man then slowly moves his bent legs in the air and brings them down one by one. He sits on the sand, his eyes on the horizon.

BN's shoes, scattered by the trampling feet, lie orphaned. This morning's polished leather now muddied and somewhat cracked.

The water rocks a lone sock hither and thither; its mate is nowhere in sight.

STEPHANIE HEIT

UNDERWATER PLOT TO GET THE RAFT BACK

underwater plot to get the raft back   (displaced muskrat gathers cohorts)
    birds in various costumes   red shoulder pads   black shift –
yellow chest medallion   sand siphons into my limbs   her breathing
(deepens)   dock's bleached wood   we touch & scan our pre-
    evolution tails

JIM DANIELS

I LIKE WATCHING RIVERS

I'm not fussy. Any body

of rushing water. 3oo miles away,

my parents meet with a brief-cased

man to settle their affairs on the way

out the door, so we don't kill each other

trying to do it ourselves—us, the kids,

and it, divide the meager spoils

with the clawed hands of grudge.

We ourselves get ready to retire,

take the package, shred the paper,

wave goodbye when appropriate

or give the finger, or both. The river

never waves good-bye. The Monongahela

after spring rain—high water ripples

and brown churn beneath the surface.

I hear that long-gone fish are returning

to cleaner waters. Long-gone faith

in returning. Going against the current

has never been our style. My parents,

nervous to meet the man, relieved when it's over.

They're blowing in the wind, but holding on

to the clothesline. Lists shorten

in my father's neat script. My blind mother

scrawls in overlapping hieroglyphics

we try to decipher when the mailman

guesses right and drops her letters into

our hearts. We've got to name our rivers,

but I like to think of them as one constant

unnamed thing in the face of all we name,

in the face of calculated distance. The man

with the briefcase is headed my way.

I know everybody has a lot to say

about rivers, and dying.

Today, I'm just watching.

MICHAEL LISIESKI

NIGHT OWLS

It smelled like cigarettes
in the middle of nothing.
My love is asleep with her love
and the highway
almost put to bed.

We were drinking mezcal in Detroit.
We were drinking something like stars:
the points of light jumping from their faces,
how she left trails between him and me,
each waiting for her head to settle.

The final touch: that thistle plant
mutant, the many stems fused and ribbon-like.
The other joinings: notes slipped between us,
gone to seed. His hand on my neck,
the new smell of his breath

and the ways we learned
to pass the aeons
she spent in the bathroom,
getting herself ready
for who knows what.

ELIZABETH KERLIKOWSKE

THE SIXTH DECADE OF SPRING CLEANING

I spent dusting light fixtures and cleaning
bulbs. I needed to be near or, better, in the
light. Glass globes freed of bug husks and
indiscriminate specks. Balanced on an end
table, I cradled the ceiling dome in one hand,
unscrewed three screws a quarter inch. Wash,
rinse, repeat to reinstall. Living room bulbs
I'd never unscrewed. Bulbs above the stove I
had to clean with vinegar. New-fangled bulbs
I was afraid to touch; they didn't look like
ideas. Bulbs allergic to human skin, our
depraved oils. I did what I could. I began in
the bedroom and ended there. My last day.
I wanted to leave the place well-lit. Every
exhibit is worth seeing.

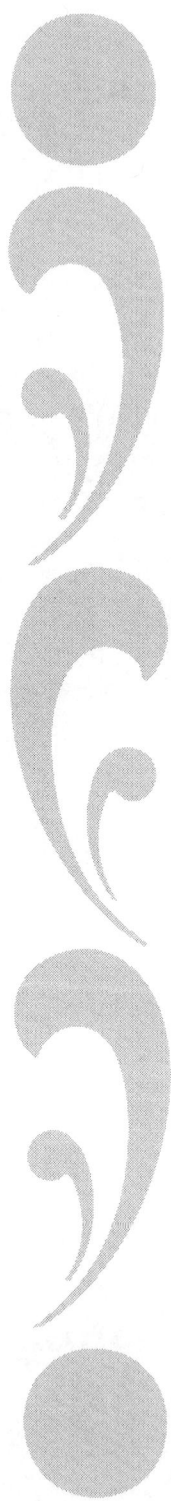

CONTRIBUTORS

CATHERINE ANDERSON is the author of *Woman with a Gambling Mania* (Mayapple Press), *The Work of Hands* (Perugia Press) and *In the Mother Tongue* (Alice James Books). Her poems have appeared in the *I-70 Review*, *Crab Orchard Review*, *The Southern Review* and others. Born in Detroit, she lived in the Boston area for two decades and now lives in Kansas City where she works with the region's refugee communities.

MICHAEL BARTELT is a high school English teacher and basketball coach who makes poems.

ANNA BERNSTEIN is a historical research assistant specializing in women's history. Her work has appeared in *Concho River Review*, *apt, decomP magazinE,* and *Inch*, among others. She has two identical cats and currently lives in Brooklyn, like everyone else who grew up in Manhattan.

After 20 years in and around California, **JOHN F. BUCKLEY** once again lives in Ann Arbor, Michigan with his wife. His publications include various poems, two chapbooks, the collection *Sky Sandwiches*, and, with Martin Ott, *Poets' Guide to America* and *Yankee Broadcast Network*. His website is www.johnfbuckley.net.

PATRICIA CLARK has published poetry in *Slate, The Atlantic, Gettysburg Review, Seattle Review*, and in several books of poetry, most recently *The Canopy* (2017) and *Sunday Rising* (2013). Her fiction has appeared in the *2016 Write Michigan Anthology*.

DENNIS CUMMINGS lives in Poway, California, where he collects stray golf balls and pre-1970 coins. He wrote "Armadillo" after reading an article in *National Geographic* about our disappearing species. Growing up in San Diego, he remembers often coming across the marvelous horned toad (actually a lizard) as he walked to school — always ready for a "duck and cover" response to the ever-present threat of a nuclear attack. Sadly, the horned toad has become scarce as hen's teeth.

JIM DANIELS is the author of sixteen poetry books, including his most recent, *Rowing Inland* (Wayne State University Press, 2017), and the forthcoming *Street Calligraphy* (Steel Toe Books). *The End of Blessings*, the fourth short film he has written and produced, appeared in numerous film festivals in 2016. A native of Detroit, Daniels is the Thomas Stockham University Professor of English at Carnegie Mellon University.

MERRIDAWN DUCKLER is a poet and playwright from Portland, Oregon whose recent poetry is published or forthcoming in *TAB* (nominated for Best of the Net), *Fifth Wednesday, The Offing, Literary Orphans, Whistling Shade, International Psychoanalysis, Unbroken,* and *interrupture.* Her fellowships and awards include Writers@Work, NEA, Yaddo, Squaw Valley, SLS St. Petersburg, Russia, and the Southampton Poetry Conference. She is an editor at *Narrative* and the international philosophy journal *Evental Aesthetics.*

A lifelong resident of Michigan, **CJ GIROUX** is an associate professor of English at Saginaw Valley State University, where he also serves as the assistant director of the school's Writing Center. He is the author of the chapbook *Destination: Michigan.*

JONATHAN GREENHAUSE was the winner of Kind of a Hurricane Press's 2015 Editor's Choice Poetry Award, the 2nd-prize winner in the 2016 *Gemini Magazine* Poetry Open, a finalist for this year's *Green Mountains Review* Book Prize, a finalist for Soundings East's 2016 Claire Keyes Award in Poetry, and a finalist for the 2016 *Iowa Review Poetry Award.* A four-time nominee for the Pushcart Prize, he is also a past contributor to *Dunes Review.*

ED HACK was a teacher and is now a poet. He has written poetry for years, free verse mostly, until the last three years, when he started writing metered poetry, trying to find a new music, new kinds of precision, and, hopefully, depth, within a traditional form, the sonnet.

A native of Israel, **RINAT HAREL** moved to the U.S. in 1991. With a bachelor's and master's degrees in fine art, she studied creative writing at Emerson College. Her work focuses on Israel's social, political, and cultural challenges. She is currently working on a fictional memoir entailing her experience as an operations-room sergeant in an Israeli Air-Force squadron. Rinat's work has been published in magazines such as the *East Coast Ink*, *The Masters Review*, *Consequences Magazine*, and *Canyon Voices*.

STEPHANIE HEIT is a poet, dancer, and teacher of somatic writing, contemplative dance practice, and kundalini yoga. She lives with bipolar disorder and is a member of the Olimpias, an international disability-performance collective. *The Color She Gave Gravity* (The Operating System, 2017) is her first book, and her work most recently appeared in *Midwestern Gothic*, *Typo*, *Streetnotes*, *Nerve Lantern*, *Queer Disability Anthology*, *Spoon Knife Anthology*, and *Theatre Topics*. She lives in Ann Arbor, Michigan.

KAREN PAUL HOLMES has a full-length collection, *Untying the Knot* (Aldrich Press, 2014). Publications include *Prairie Schooner*, *Poet Lore*, *Poetry East*, *Atlanta Review*, *Slipstream*, and *Best Emerging Poets 2015* (Stay Thirsty Media, 2016). To support fellow writers, Holmes originated and hosts a critique group in Atlanta, and Writers' Night Out in the Blue Ridge Mountains. She grew up in Michigan and has an MA in music history from the University of Michigan.

D. R. JAMES'S poetry collections are *Since Everything Is All I've Got* (March Street, 2011) and five chapbooks, most recently *Why War* and *Split-Level* (Finishing Line 2014, 2017). Poems have appeared in various journals and anthologies, including *Poems in Michigan / Michigan in Poetry* (New Issues, 2013). James lives in Saugatuck, Michigan, and has been teaching writing, literature, and peace-making at Hope College for going on 32 years.

SONJA JOHANSON has recent work appearing in the *Best American Poetry* blog, *BOAAT*, *Epiphany*, and *The Writer's Almanac*. She is a contributing editor at the *Found Poetry Review*, and the author of *Impossible Dovetail* (IDES, Silver Birch Press), *all those ragged scars* (Choose the Sword Press), and *Trees in Our Dooryards* (Redbird Chapbooks). Sonja divides her time between work in Massachusetts and her home in the mountains of western Maine. Follow her work at www.sonjajohanson.net.

YUKARI KAIHORI was born in Japan and grew up shifting from Asia to South America to North America. She creates paintings to examine the intersections between the physical and internal landscapes, with a special focus on how those landscapes interact with memory and imagination. Yukari earned her B.A. in studio art in 2004 from Lewis and Clark College in Oregon. She has lived and worked from her studio in New Zealand since 2011. In 2015, Yukari received a Pollock Krasner Foundation Grant award. See more of her work at www.yukari-kaihori.com

ELIZABETH KERLIKOWSKE is president of Friends of Poetry, a nonprofit dedicated to bringing people and poetry together. Her most recent chapbook is *Chain of Lakes*, a letterpress book from the Kalamazoo Book Arts Center.

PETER KRUMBACH was born in what used to be Czechoslovakia. Shortly after graduating with a degree in visual arts, he left the country and began a journey that eventually took him to New York. He worked in commercial art and later as a translator and broadcaster. His poems have recently appeared or are forthcoming in such places as *Alaska Quarterly Review*, *Phoebe*, *RHINO*, *Columbia Poetry Review*, and *Fugue*. He lives in La Jolla, California.

KRIS KUNZ graduated from the University of Michigan and has a master's degree in English literature from Oakland University. Her poetry has appeared in *Dunes Review* and *Scintilla Magazine*, and she was awarded the William J. Shaw Memorial Prize for Poetry in 2014. Her chapbook, *Crime Story*, was published by Michigan Writers Cooperative Press in 2015. She taught in the Detroit area and now lives and writes in Frankfort, Michigan with her dog, horses, and husband.

PETRA KUPPERS is a disability culture activist, a community performance artist, and a professor at the University of Michigan, Ann Arbor. Her most recent poetry collection is *PearlStitch* (Spuyten Duyvil, 2016). Her stories appear in *Sycamore Review*, *Future Fire*, *Capricious*, *Festival Writer*, *PodCastle*, and *Accessing the Future*. She is the artistic director of The Olimpias, an international disability culture collective. She lives in Ann Arbor with her partner and collaborator, Stephanie Heit. Find her online at www. petrakuppersfiction.wordpress.com.

ANNA LEAHY'S books include *Aperture, Generation Space: A Love Story, Tumor,* and *Constituents of Matter.* Her essays won the top prizes at *Ninth Letter* and *Dogwood* in 2016 and were Notables in *The Best American Essays* 2013 and 2016. She teaches in the MFA and BFA programs at Chapman University, where she curates the Tabula Poetica reading series and edits *TAB: A Journal of Poetry & Poetics.* www.generationspace.com

MICHAEL LISIESKI was born in Ohio, grew up in western Pennsylvania, and attended college in Buffalo. He now lives in Detroit with three cats, two rabbits, and one of his partners, and studies neuroscience. His poems appear or are forthcoming in *Midwestern Gothic, Star*Line, Passages North, The Cape Rock*, and other journals.

TODD MERCER won the Dyer-Ives Kent County Prize for Poetry (2016), the National Writers Series Poetry Prize (2016) and the Grand Rapids Festival Flash Fiction Award (2015). His digital chapbook, *Life-wish Maintenance,* appeared at *Right Hand Pointing.* His poetry and fiction appear in *100 Word Story, Dogzplot, The Ekphrastic Review, Eunoia Review, EXPOUND, Flash Fiction Magazine. Fried Chicken and Coffee, Gnarled Oak, The Lake, Literary Orphans, Main Street Rag Anthologies, Split Lip Magazine, Star 82 Review,* and *Two Cities Review.*

REBECCA OET is a high-school student from Solon, Ohio. She enjoys reading fiction and comic books, writing short stories and poetry, and watching anime. Rebecca is a national silver medalist for photography in the 2015 Scholastic Art & Writing Awards and has won gold and silver keys for poetry in the Regional Scholastic Writing Competition & Exhibition. Her poetry appears in *Teen Ink Magazine, Freshwater Literary Journal, Zingara Poet* and the Summer 2014 *National Poetry Contest Anthology.*

ALAINA PEPIN is a poet and writer born and raised on Lake Superior's shore in Michigan's Upper Peninsula. She is in the midst of her fourth and final year as an English secondary education major at Northern Michigan University and will be student teaching in the winter semester. Her poetry appears in *Rust+Moth, Beech Street Review, Pif Magazine, Sink Hollow Literary Journal,* and *Ore Ink Review.*

ADAM SCHEFFLER'S first book of poems, *A Dog's Life*, was selected by Denise Duhamel as the winner of the Jacar Press Poetry Book Contest and was published in 2016. His poems have appeared in *The American Poetry Review, The Antioch Review, Rattle, North American Review, Verse Daily*, and many other venues. He grew up in California, received his MFA in poetry from the Iowa Writers' Workshop, and is currently finishing his PhD in English at Harvard.

R. THOMAS SHEARDY, a lifelong resident of Michigan, lives in Crockery Township. He has been writing most of his life, both fiction and for his profession, but is only recently published. His work has most recently appeared in the *Write Michigan 2016* anthology. A retired professor of art history, he has done archaeological work in the jungles of Yucatan and is an avid traveler. He is also an artist, maintains a large English garden, and raises orchids.

BRENDAN SHERRY lives and works in Nashville, Tennessee.

DANIEL STEWART is by training an historian and by profession a print and book designer and occasional radio producer, as well as a writer of memoir and fiction (which he tries to keep from overlapping). In other words, most of what he does is related to the telling of good and true stories. He has lived with his wife, Amanda Holmes, in Leelanau County, Michigan, since 2004.

ANDREW SZILVASY teaches British literature outside of Boston and currently has poems in *Modern Poetry Quarterly Review, Shot Glass Journal, Boston Accent Lit,* and *Asses of Parnassus*, among others. He lives in Boston with his wife and two cats. Aside from writing, reading and teaching, Andrew spends his time hiking and brewing beer.

DIZ WARNER has enjoyed an eclectic writing career. She was a frequent humor columnist for *The Seattle Post-Intelligencer*, and is a contributor to the books, *The Sixties Chronicle* and *The Civil Rights Chronicle: The African-American Struggle for Freedom*. Originally a Michigan poet, she is currently working on short stories and a novella and is a recent alumna of The Sirenland Conference in Positano, Italy. She earns her living ghostwriting policy articles and books.

KIRK WESTPHAL is originally from Michigan, and now lives near Boston where he works as a water supply consultant. His poems have appeared in past issues of *Dunes Review*, *The Road Not Taken*, and *Albatross*, and he has also read on *National Public Radio*. In 2015, he published his first book, *No Ordinary Game*. To inspire further writing, he is building a cabin in the hills of Western Massachusetts along a trout stream.

JOANNA WHITE, a music professor, studies poetry with Robert Fanning and Jeffrey Bean, fiction with Darrin Doyle, and has works appearing in *Examined Life Journal, Healing Muse, Measure, Sow's Ear Poetry Review, The MacGuffin, Ars Medica, The Cape Rock, Chariton Review, Hummingbird, Pulse, Temenos, KYSO Flash Anthology #2, Minerva Rising Literary Journal*, and the *Naugatuck River Review*. She lives in Mount Pleasant, Michigan with her husband and has a daughter and son in college.

CALL FOR PATRONS

Michigan Writers is a non-profit endeavor to promote creative work within the northern Michigan community and beyond.

The cost of publication can be underwritten in part by individual contributions. We invite you to support the publication of the Summer/Fall 2017 issue with a donation of $25.

Send your check payable to Michigan Writers to:

P.O. Box 2355
Traverse City, MI 49685

Thank you in advance for your support.

DUNES REVIEW
SUBMISSION GUIDELINES

We welcome submissions from anyone, anywhere, although we do encourage Michigan writers to join or renew your membership ($40 annually, which includes a two-issue annual subscription to *Dunes Review*). Learn more about Michigan Writers and the benefits of membership at MICHWRITERS.ORG/JOIN. Please "Like" us on Facebook to receive notices about upcoming events, workshops, and readings.

All work must be sent via DUNESREVIEW.SUBMITTABLE. COM. We do not accept submissions via email or postal mail. You will need to have a Submittable.com account to send work. Creating an account is free and you can easily keep track of your submissions from within your account.

All work received during the reading periods will be read. Response times will vary, but we make every effort to respond within 90 days of receipt. If you have not received a response after 120 days, please contact us by email at dunesreview@michwriters.org. Our next reading period runs from May 1 — August 1, 2017.

Please send no more than one submission in a given genre while a decision from us is outstanding, and send work no more than twice per reading period. Simultaneous submissions (the same work sent to multiple journals) are fine, but leave a note in Submittable immediately if your work is accepted elsewhere.

Payment for work comes in the form of two copies of the print journal.

We consider:

- Poetry (up to 4 poems; please format and submit as a single .doc, .docx, or .rtf document, one poem per page)
- Short fiction or creative nonfiction (3,000-word maximum)

We do not consider:

- Previously published material
- Academic writing or journalism
- Unsolicited reviews or interviews

More detailed guidelines can be found at DUNESREVIEW. SUBMITTABLE.COM.

Made in the USA
Lexington, KY
24 March 2017